Lives and Times

# Samuel Morse

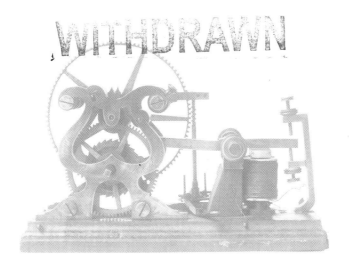

M. C. Hall

Heinemann Library
Chicago, Illinois

Customer Service  888-454-2279
Visit our website at www.heinemannlibrary.com

Page layout by Cherylyn Bredemann
Photo research by Bill Broyles

Printed and bound in Hong Kong and China by South China Printing Co Ltd

08 07 06 05 04
10 9 8 7 6 5 4 3 2 1

**Library of Congress
Cataloging-in-Publication Data**
Samuel Morse / M. C. Hall.
ISBN 1-4034-5329-2 (HC), 1-4034-5337-3 (Pbk.)
The Cataloging-in-Publication Data for this title is on file with the Library of Congress.

**Acknowledgments**
The author and publishers are grateful to the following for permission to reproduce copyright material: Title page, pp. 14, 15, 23 Bettmann/Corbis; icon, p. 21 (Morse Code) Heinemann Library; icon (artist palette) PhotoDisc/Getty Images; p. 4 Scott Braut/Heinemann Library; pp. 5, 7, 17, 20, 26 Library of Congress; p. 6 National Museum of American History/Smithsonian Institution, Washington, D. C.; p. 8 Corbis; p. 9 National Portrait Gallery/Smithsonian Institution/Art Resource, NY; p. 10 Smithsonian American Art Museum, Washington DC/Art Resource. NY; pp. 11, 18 Mary Evans Picture Library; p. 12 Mead Art Museum, Amherst College, Bequest of Herbert L. Pratt (Class of 1895), AC 1945.78; p. 13 Superstock; p. 16 Courtesy The National Academy of Design; p. 19 New York University Archives; pp. 22, 24 Hulton-Deutsch Collection/Corbis; p. 25 Dennis Szeba/Morse Historic Site; p. 27 Bill Broyles/Slick-O Productions; p. 28 Albert J. Blodgett/Morse Historic Site; p. 29 Underwood and Underwood/Corbis

Cover photographs by (top left) Heinemann Library, (bottom left) Bettmann/Corbis, (bottom right) Library of Congress

The publisher would like to thank Charly Rimsa for her comments in the preparation of this book.

Every effort has been made to contact copyright holders of any material reproduced in this book. Any omissions will be rectified in subsequent printings if notice is given to the publisher.

Some words are shown in bold, **like this.** You can find out what they mean by looking in the glossary.

# Contents

# Sending Messages

Today, it is easy for people to **communicate.** Airplanes carry letters across the country in a few hours. People talk on the telephone. Radios and televisions spread news quickly.

Many people today carry cellular phones everywhere they go.

Long ago, messages and letters traveled by horse, train, or boat. It took weeks or months to send news across the country. Then, Samuel Morse had an idea that made communication faster.

This photo of Samuel was taken in about 1850.

# The Early Years

Samuel Morse was born in Charlestown, Massachusetts, on April 27, 1791. He was the first child in his family. Samuel had two younger brothers named Sidney and Richard.

This painting shows Samuel (second from the left) and his family.

Samuel's father was a **minister** and a writer. Both of Samuel's parents thought learning was important. When Samuel was seven years old, he went away to live at a **boarding school.**

Samuel wrote this journal page when he was thirteen years old.

# Working and Learning

When Samuel was fourteen years old, he went to Yale College in Connecticut. Samuel's favorite classes were art and science. He was excited to learn about electricity. It was a new discovery.

Yale College is now called Yale University.

Samuel painted this picture of himself in about 1812.

After he finished college in 1810, Samuel wanted to go to **Europe** to study art. But his parents thought drawing and painting were a waste of time. They wanted Samuel to sell books instead.

# Off to Europe

Samuel went home to Massachusetts. He worked at a bookstore during the day. He painted at night. Soon his parents saw how important art was to Samuel. They said he could go to **Europe** to study.

Samuel painted this picture called *The Goldfish Bowl* in about 1835.

This is an art show at the Royal Academy of Art in London, where Samuel took art classes.

In 1811 Samuel sailed to London, England. He took art classes there. Samuel even won a medal for a statue he made. But he ran out of money. He came home to Massachusetts in 1815.

# Working as a Painter

There were no cameras in Samuel's time. People hired artists to paint their **portraits.** So Samuel traveled around, working as a painter. In 1816 Samuel met Lucretia Walker. They were married two years later.

Samuel painted this picture of Lucretia.

Samuel painted this portrait for money in about 1824.

By 1823 Samuel and Lucretia had a son and a daughter. Samuel still traveled to paint portraits of people. He had a hard time making enough money as a painter.

# Early Inventions

Samuel and his brother invented this water pump for firefighters.

Samuel looked for ways to make more money. He and his brother Sidney invented a water pump for firefighters to use. Samuel also invented a machine to cut **marble** for statues.

Samuel painted this picture called *The House of Representatives*.

Samuel did not earn much money from his inventions. But he did start to be known as an excellent **portrait** painter. He was asked to paint pictures of important people and places.

# Sad Times

In 1825 Samuel and Lucretia had another son. Lucretia died a month later. Samuel was sad and lonely. He moved to New York City.

Samuel and other artists set up the National Academy of Design to help artists in New York City.

In 1829 Samuel decided to spend more time studying art. He sold his belongings and his house. He left his three children with family members. Then, he returned to **Europe.**

In his journal, Samuel made notes about art he saw in Europe.

# A New Idea

In France Samuel saw something new. Signals on top of tall towers were used to send messages. In bad weather, no one could see the signals. Samuel thought there must be a better way to do things.

This old picture shows how the signal on top of a building could send messages.

18

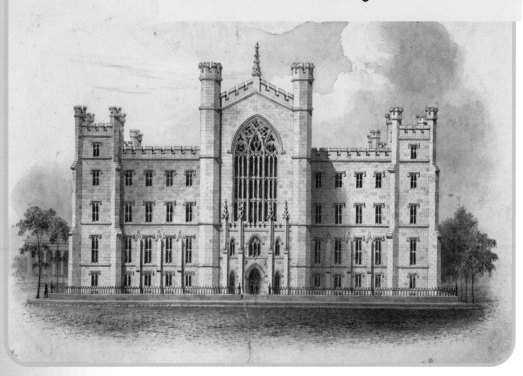

Samuel lived and taught in one of the towers of this building.

In 1832 Samuel sailed back to New York City to teach art. On the ship, he heard people talking about how electricity traveled through wires. He wondered if a message could travel along a wire, too.

# The First Telegraph

Samuel invented a machine he called a telegraph. He also invented a **code** of dots and dashes. By starting and stopping the electricity, Samuel used the code to send an **electronic** message along the wire.

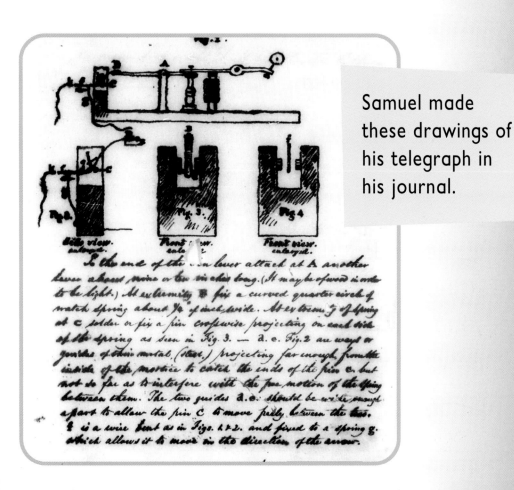

Samuel made these drawings of his telegraph in his journal.

Morse code uses dots and dashes to stand for letters, numbers, and some punctuation.

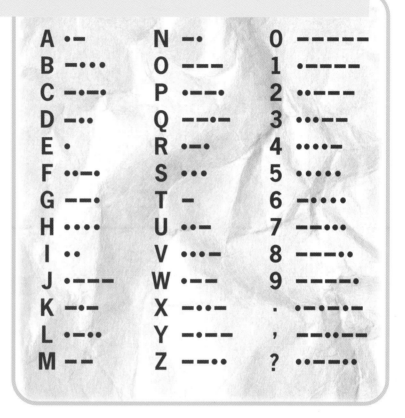

| | | | | | |
|---|---|---|---|---|---|
| A | ·— | N | —· | 0 | —————— |
| B | —··· | O | ——— | 1 | ·———— |
| C | —·—· | P | ·——· | 2 | ··——— |
| D | —·· | Q | ——·— | 3 | ···—— |
| E | · | R | ·—· | 4 | ····— |
| F | ··—· | S | ··· | 5 | ····· |
| G | ——· | T | — | 6 | —···· |
| H | ···· | U | ··— | 7 | ——··· |
| I | ·· | V | ···— | 8 | ———·· |
| J | ·——— | W | ·—— | 9 | ————· |
| K | —·— | X | —··— | . | ·—·—·— |
| L | ·—·· | Y | —·—— | , | ——··—— |
| M | —— | Z | ——·· | ? | ··——·· |

Samuel found some **business partners** who helped him improve his invention. In 1838 he showed the telegraph to people in the U.S. **government.** It sent a message a short distance.

# A Successful Invention

This photograph shows Samuel in 1850.

Samuel thought a telegraph could send messages a long way. He kept working on it. In 1843 **Congress** gave Samuel money to build a **telegraph line** between Baltimore, Maryland, and Washington, D.C.

Telegraph messages traveled many miles in just a few minutes.

On May 24, 1844, Samuel sent the first telegraph message from Washington, D.C., to Baltimore. People were excited about his invention. Soon telegraph lines connected other big cities, too.

# The Later Years

Samuel's invention made him rich. In 1847 he bought a large house and some land near Poughkeepsie, New York. The next year Samuel married Sarah Griswold. Samuel and Sarah had four children.

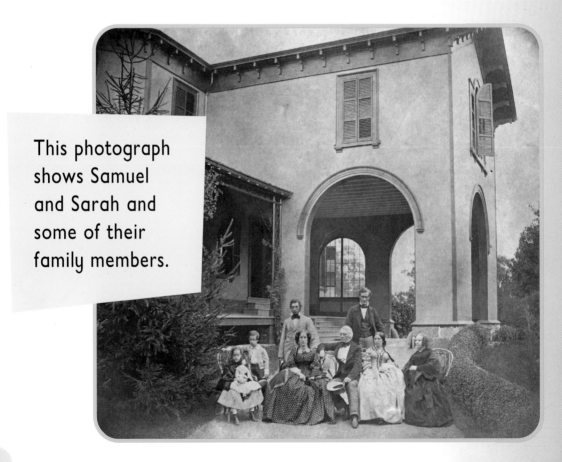

This photograph shows Samuel and Sarah and some of their family members.

This photo shows the gardens at Samuel's home.

Samuel called his home Locust Grove.
He fixed the house and made it larger.
He put in beautiful gardens. The house
even had a tall tower that gave Samuel
a view of the Hudson River.

# Sharing His Success

This photograph shows Samuel in his old age.

Samuel wanted to help others. He gave money to schools. He helped young artists by giving them money while they studied art.

People wanted to honor Samuel for his work. In 1871 a statue of him was put in Central Park in New York City. The next year Samuel died at the age of 81.

This statue of Samuel still stands in Central Park.

# Learning More About Samuel Morse

In 1963 Samuel's home at Locust Grove became a **national historic landmark.** People can visit it to learn about him.

Visitors to Locust Grove can see some of Samuel's paintings and inventions.

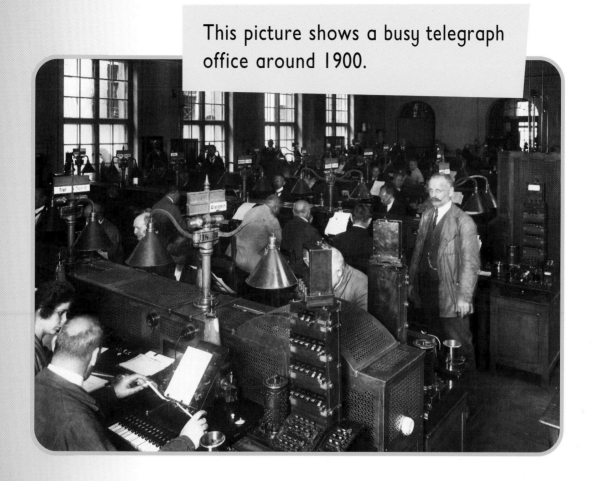

This picture shows a busy telegraph office around 1900.

Today, there are faster ways to send messages than by telegraph. But people are still interested in the **code** Samuel invented. There are Morse code clubs and telegraph clubs around the world.

## Fact File

- Samuel Morse was one of the first Americans to make daguerreotypes, an early kind of photograph.

- It took Samuel Morse eighteen months to paint a scene of the inside of the Capitol building in Washington, D.C. The painting includes 80 **portraits** of important people in the U.S. **government.**

- The words of Samuel's first telegraph message were a quotation from the Bible.

- By 1861 **telegraph lines** stretched across the United States.

## Timeline

| | |
|---|---|
| 1791 | Samuel Morse is born in Charlestown, Massachusetts. |
| 1810 | Samuel graduates from Yale and works as a bookseller. |
| 1811 | Samuel goes to **Europe** to study art. |
| 1815 | Samuel returns to the United States and begins painting portraits. |
| 1818 | Samuel marries Lucretia Pickering. |
| 1825 | Lucretia Morse dies. |
| 1829 | Samuel returns to Europe to study art. |
| 1832 | Samuel returns to the United States to teach art. |
| 1835 | Samuel makes his first telegraph. |
| 1844 | The first telegraph message is sent. |
| 1848 | Samuel marries Sarah Griswold. |
| 1872 | Samuel Morse dies. |

# Glossary

**boarding school**   school where students live during the school year

**business partner**   person who works with someone else to run a business

**code**   system in which symbols stand for something else

**communicate**   to share information

**Congress**   part of the U.S. government that passes laws

**electronic**   powered by electricity

**Europe**   one of the seven continents of the world. England and France are countries in Europe.

**government**   group of people who rule a country

**marble**   strong, smooth stone that can be carved into different shapes

**minister**   person who leads a church

**national historic landmark**   place set aside because it shows something important in the history of the United States

**portrait**   painting or drawing of a person

**telegraph line**   system of wires used to telegraph messages

## More Books to Read

**An older reader can help you with these books:**

Alter, Judy. *Samuel F. B. Morse: Inventor and Code Creator*. Chanhassen, Minn.: The Child's World, 2003.

Hossell, Karen Price. *Morse Code*. Chicago: Heinemann Library, 2002.

Zannos, Susan. *Samuel Morse and the Electric Telegraph*. Newark, Del.: Mitchell Lane, 2004.

## Index